WEIRD BUT TRUE SCIENCE

Weird But True Rocks

Series Science Consultant:
Mary Poulson, PhD
Biologist
Central Washington University
Ellensburg, WA

Series Literacy Consultant:
Allan A. De Fina, PhD
Dean, College of Education/Professor of Literacy Education
New Jersey City University
Past President of the New Jersey Reading Association

Carmen Bredeson

CONTENTS

WORDS TO KNOW

crystal (KRIS tuhl)—A type of solid that often sparkles, like ice, snowflakes, or glass. Quartz is a kind of crystal.

delicate (DEL ih kit)—Something that is easy to break.

geode (jee OHD)—A rock that has crystals on the inside.

lava (LAH vuh)—Melted rock that comes out of a volcano or an opening in the earth.

THREE TYPES OF ROCKS

IGNEOUS (IG nee uss) — Magma is melted rock below Earth's surface. Hot magma cools. It makes igneous rocks. Most of Earth's crust is made of this kind of rock.

METAMORPHIC — (meh tuh MOR fik) Deep in the earth, igneous or sedimentary rocks get very hot. Pressure builds up and squeezes the rocks. The heat and pressure change them into metamorphic rocks.

SEDIMENTARY — (sed ih MEN tuh ree) Seashells, sand, pebbles, plants, and animals sink to the bottom of lakes and oceans. Layer after layer piles up. The top layers press on the bottom layers. The pressing turns the layers into sedimentary rocks.

ROCKS CAN BE WEIRD!

Some rocks float and some rocks fizz!
Rocks can be small like a pebble.
They can be big like a mountain.
The rocks in this book are pretty weird.
You would be lucky to find one of them
in your backyard.

GEODES
Rocks with a secret sparkle

Geodes are plain brown rocks on the outside. But break one open and get ready for a surprise! They are full of sparkly **crystals.** The beautiful crystals grow in many different colors.

It's weird, but it's true!

This rock is SEDIMENTARY.

This rock is METAMORPHIC.

MARBLE
Rocks that fizz

The Taj Majal in India is made with marble.

Do you know how to tell if a rock is marble?
Drop a little vinegar or lemon juice on it.
If small bubbles appear, you have marble. *FIZZ!*
Many famous statues are made of marble.
Whole buildings are too.

It's weird, but it's true!

LAVA BOMBS
Rocks that fall from the sky

Red hot **lava** shoots out of a volcano. Up, up it goes.
Some of the lava cools as it flies through the air.
It hits the ground as solid pieces of rock.
A lava bomb can be as small as a golf
ball or bigger than a car!

It's weird, but it's true!

This rock is IGNEOUS.

This rock is SEDIMENTARY.

Hoodoos
Rocks that look a little spooky

Hoodoos are made of hard and soft rock. When wind and rain hit the rocks, parts fall away. The soft parts fall faster than the hard ones. That is why hoodoos can have such strange shapes.

It's weird, but it's true!

DINO ROCKS
My, what big feet!

Long ago, a dinosaur walked across the mud. Its feet left prints in the ground. Sun baked the prints. Dust blew and filled up the holes. The ground got hard and rocky. The prints are still there—real dinosaur tracks!

It's weird, but it's true!

This rock is SEDIMENTARY.

These tracks were made by a meat-eating dinosaur.

This rock is SEDIMENTARY.

FLINT
Rocks that spark

Hit two pieces of flint together. Watch the SPARKS fly! You can make fire with flint. American Indians used flint to make arrowheads and spear points. Flint has very sharp edges.

It's weird, but it's true!

PUMICE
Rocks that float

Throw a piece of pumice (PUH miss) in the water. Does it sink? No, pumice FLOATS! It is full of little air holes. The holes were made by gas bubbles in lava. The holes make pumice light enough to float.

It's weird, but it's true!

This rock is IGNEOUS.

DELICATE ARCH
Rocks that curve

Delicate Arch is in Utah. It was once a big rock. Wind and water made tiny holes in the rock. The holes got bigger and bigger. Finally there was just one big hole in the middle of the rock. Only the arch was left.

It's weird, but its true!

This rock is SEDIMENTARY.

LEARN MORE

Books

Gray, Susan. *Dinosaur Tracks.* Children's Press. Danbury, Conn.: 2007.

Rosinsky, Natalie. *Rocks: Hard, Soft, Smooth, and Rough.* Mankato, Minn.: Picture Window Books, 2004.

Wallace, Nancy Elizabeth. *Rocks! Rocks! Rocks!* Tarrytown, N.Y.: Marshall Cavendish, 2009.

LEARN MORE

Web Sites

Children's Museum of Indianapolis: Geo Mysteries
www.childrensmuseum.org/geomysteries/faqs.html

NASA: Earth Science for Kids
http://kids.earth.nasa.gov

INDEX

To our wonderful grandchildren: Andrew, Charlie, Kate, and Caroline

Enslow Elementary, an imprint of Enslow Publishers, Inc.

Enslow Elementary® is a registered trademark of Enslow Publishers, Inc.

Copyright © 2012 by Carmen Bredeson

Library of Congress Cataloging-in-Publication Data
Bredeson, Carmen.
  Weird but true rocks / Carmen Bredeson.
    p. cm. — (Weird but true science)
  Includes index.
  Summary: "Read about different types of rocks like lava bombs, geodes, hoodoos, and moon rocks"—Provided by publisher.
  ISBN 978-0-7660-3864-6
  1. Rocks—Miscellanea—Juvenile literature. I. Title.
  QE432.2.B74 2011
  552—dc22
                                    2010035862
Paperback ISBN 978-1-59845-370-6

Printed in China

052011 Leo Paper Group, Heshan City, Guangdong, China

10 9 8 7 6 5 4 3 2 1

To Our Readers: We have done our best to make sure all Internet addresses in this book were active and appropriate when we went to press. However, the author and the publisher have no control over and assume no liability for the material available on those Internet sites or on other Web sites they may link to. Any comments or suggestions can be sent by e-mail to comments@enslow.com or to the address on the back cover.

Photo Credits: Alamy: © Phil Cawley, p. 16, © Ted Foxx, p. 8; © Bob Walters and Jeff Breeden, p. 14; iStockphoto.com: © Debbie Lund, p. 17 (top), © Jesus Ayala, p. 3 (top), © Justin McDonald, p. 4 (bottom), © oscarshost, p. 17 (bottom); © Jupiterimages Corporation, p. 7; Photolibrary: © De Agostini Editore, p. 19, © imagebroker.net, p. 11; Photo Researchers, Inc.: © Carlyn Iverson, pp. 3 (bottom), 10, © Diccon Alexander, p. 6, © Francois Gohier, p. 15, © Sheila Terry, p. 18; Shutterstock.com, pp. 1, 2, 3 (two middle), 4 (top, middle), 5, 9, 12, 13, 17 (middle), 21.

Cover Photo: Shutterstock.com

Note to Parents and Teachers: The *Weird But True Science* series supports the National Science Education Standards for K–4 science. The Words to Know section introduces subject-specific vocabulary words, including pronunciation and definitions. Early readers may need help with these new words.

Enslow Elementary
an imprint of
Enslow Publishers, Inc.
40 Industrial Road
Box 398
Berkeley Heights, NJ 07922
USA
      http://www.enslow.com